# THE WAY OF ST. JAMES PRAYER BOOK

# THE WAY OF ST. JAMES PRAYER BOOK

BENJAMIN R. DOOLITTLE

RESOURCE *Publications* • Eugene, Oregon

THE WAY OF ST. JAMES PRAYER BOOK

Copyright © 2019 Benjamin R. Doolittle. All rights reserved. Except for brief quotations in critical publications or reviews, no part of this book may be reproduced in any manner without prior written permission from the publisher. Write: Permissions, Wipf and Stock Publishers, 199 W. 8th Ave., Suite 3, Eugene, OR 97401.

Resource Publications
An Imprint of Wipf and Stock Publishers
199 W. 8th Ave., Suite 3
Eugene, OR 97401

www.wipfandstock.com

PAPERBACK ISBN: 978-1-5326-7733-5
HARDCOVER ISBN: 978-1-5326-7734-2
EBOOK ISBN: 978-1-5326-7735-9

Manufactured in the U.S.A.  02/19/19

To my beloved, the hand in my hand, and
To my beloved mermaids

# CONTENTS

INTRODUCTION | ix
THE LORD'S PRAYER | 1
SUNDAY MORNING | 2
SUNDAY MID-DAY | 5
SUNDAY EVENING | 7
MONDAY MORNING | 10
MONDAY MID-DAY | 13
MONDAY EVENING | 15
TUESDAY MORNING | 18
TUESDAY MID-DAY | 22
TUESDAY EVENING | 24
WEDNESDAY MORNING | 28
WEDNESDAY MID-DAY | 31
WEDNESDAY EVENING | 33
THURSDAY MORNING | 36
THURSDAY MID-DAY | 39
THURSDAY EVENING | 41
FRIDAY MORNING | 44
FRIDAY MID-DAY | 47

FRIDAY EVENING | 49

SATURDAY MORNING | 51

SATURDAY MID-DAY | 56

SATURDAY EVENING | 58

COMPLINE ~ A prayer for the close of the day | 61

PRAYERS FOR THE DAY OF ARRIVAL
TO SANTIAGO DE COMPOSTELA

MORNING | 63

MID-DAY | 66

EVENING | 68

# INTRODUCTION

The Way of St. James has a enduring draw for the modern seeker. The Way is more than 1300 years old. Pilgrims have been seeking God, seeking answers, and seeking absolution ever since the relics of St. James were discovered in the early 9th century. Yet, the pilgrimage is decidedly modern. Amidst the busyness of modern life, we have a deep yearning to unplug from the noise of email, news feeds, and social media and to reconnect with ancient practices. We ache to reconnect with God. In this sense, not much has changed.

The Way of St. James is different from a hike or a vacation. You are not a tourist. You are not outside history looking in, the way you are when you visit the Louvre or the Pantheon. Instead, you enter *into* history. You enter into the stream of every pilgrim who has gone before and will come after you. You belong to the lineage of the medieval king who journeyed with his retinue, the leper who sought healing, and the weary seeker who seeks peace. These are your people. The Way is now your story too.

You sacrifice much to join the Camino. You give up one thing for another. You could go to the beach, attend a family reunion, or connect with friends. You could continue in your work or do more chores around the home, but you feel a tug, a nudge, for something deeper. And you will discover that which you need.

My humble advice is to unplug. There is so much noise in the world—the constant barrage of news feeds, the river of social media, the constancy of emails. This practice is the addiction of

## INTRODUCTION

modernity. We feel anxious when we forget our phones. We feel a compulsion to constantly check in. The cloud of noise distracts us from seeking God. We are filled, but often filled with junk food. We crave a satisfying meal. This pilgrimage is the opportunity for solid food, a drink that satisfies every thirst.

My second piece of advice is to bring a journal. Think. Reflect. Pray. Imagine. Journaling is an exercise of mindfulness, of entering into the experience more deeply. How is God working into your heart as you hike? How has an interaction with a fellow pilgrim shaped your outlook? How is your body responding to the hard work of the trail? All of this shapes our faith. Journaling chronicles our ongoing conversation with God.

The real challenge to the Way of St. James is, "What next?" Upon returning to your old life, you will be different. You will have known sore muscles, weary long days, and deep joys of contemplation. You will have lived simply. You will have created a new rhythm in your life of prayer and contemplation. How do you preserve this as you re-enter your prior world? How can you instill the lesson of the Way into the rhythm of work, family, and life? This is very hard to do, given the cacophony of modern life. Each of us answers these questions differently, but I believe part of the answer is *that we must invest time*. Like any loving relationship, we strengthened our relationship with God by spending time with God. This is the realm of spiritual disciplines – the divine office, contemplative prayer, lectio divina, and the like. There is a great feast of beautiful spiritual traditions. My suggestion is to try them and find your own pilgrim rhythm for yourself. Perhaps this prayer book is a start.

My hope is that this prayer book will help you invite God as a companion on your journey. The Way is hard – maybe the hardest physical adventure you have ever taken. The prayers, the scriptures will rest in your heart and mind as good company in your breathing, your sweating, and your striving. May you soak in these ancient words as you soak in the sun of northern Spain. As the physical exertion shapes you, purifies you, let these prayers do the same. You are in good company.

## INTRODUCTION

This prayer book has a balanced structure. The morning lessons highlight special moments in the gospels with reflections from classic sources and a traditional blessing. The mid-day prayer serves as a brief thanksgiving. Since this is a pilgrimage to the relics of St. James, the mid-day prayers highlight those moments in the Gospels and Acts where James is featured. For evening prayer, I include reflections from contemporary sources. Throughout, the prayers, collects, and reflections highlight themes of pilgrimage, hope, and exploration.

One challenge for this prayer book was to determine how long it would be. This is a traveling book, meant to be easy to follow, light enough for a backpack, and accessible to all within a broad Christian tradition. If you begin at St. Jean Pied de Port in France, the pilgrimage could take 35 days, and maybe more. If you choose to hike the minimum 100 kilometers to qualify for a Compostela, you may need only 4 or 5 days. A happy medium is one week. And so, you start on the day you begin your pilgrimage and follow the days of the week accordingly. There are prayers for morning, mid-day, and evening during your journey, with a compline prayer to be read upon going to sleep. There is also a day of prayer for when you arrive in Santiago.

Another challenge for prayer books is whether to use the singular "I" or the plural "we." While the Way is a solo endeavor and intensely reflective, we belong to a community of souls, the church universal. When we pray, we join the prayers of all those who raise their voices to God in thanksgiving and in hope. And so, when we pray on the Way, we join those voices with "we." The hope is that these prayers are accessible and will deepen your experience on your pilgrimage.

Finally, please realize that these words are not my own. I have arranged scripture verses, ancient prayers, and reflections from sages. None of which have come from my pen. The few collects that I have written were given to me by the trail. My proceeds from this book will be given to charity to support initiatives that deepen the contemplative life of the church.

# THE LORD'S PRAYER

Our Father,
Who art in heaven
Hallowed be thy name
Thy kingdom come
Thy will be done
On earth as it is in heaven.

Give us this day our daily bread.
Forgive us our trespasses
As we forgive those who trespass against us.
Lead us not into temptation,
But deliver us from evil.

For thine is the kingdom,
the power,
and the glory forever,
Amen.

# SUNDAY MORNING

**Invitation**

Let us run with perseverance the race that is set before us, looking to Jesus the pioneer and perfecter of our faith, who for the sake of the joy that was set before him endured the cross, disregarding its shame, and has taken his seat at the right hand of the throne of God.

Hebrews 2:1-2

**Psalm**

The Lord is my shepherd, I shall not want.
  He makes me lie down in green pastures;
he leads me beside still waters;
  he restores my soul.
He leads me in right paths
  for his name's sake.
Even though I walk through the darkest valley,
  I fear no evil;
for you are with me;
  your rod and your staff–
  they comfort me.

Psalm 23:1-4

## Collect

Almighty God, to you all hearts are open, all desires known, and from you no secrets are hid. Cleanse the thoughts of our hearts by the inspiration of your Holy Spirit, that we may perfectly love you, and worthily magnify your holy Name; through Christ our Lord. Amen.

## Lesson

Do not worry about your life, what you will eat or what you will drink, or about your body, what you will wear. Is not life more than food, and the body more than clothing? Look at the birds of the air; they neither sow nor reap nor gather into barns, and yet your heavenly Father feeds them. Are you not of more value than they? And can any of you by worrying add a single hour to your span of life? And why do you worry about clothing? Consider the lilies of the field, how they grow; they neither toil nor spin, yet I tell you, even Solomon in all his glory was not clothed like one of these. But if God so clothes the grass of the field, which is alive today and tomorrow is thrown into the oven, will he not much more clothe you—you of little faith? Therefore do not worry, saying, 'What will we eat?' or 'What will we drink?' or 'What will we wear?' For it is the Gentiles who strive for all these things; and indeed your heavenly Father knows that you need all these things. But strive first for the kingdom of God and his righteousness, and all these things will be given to you as well.

Matthew 6:25-32

## Reflection

Keep yourself as a pilgrim and stranger on the earth who has nothing to do with the affairs of the world. Keep your heart free and lifted up to God because we have here no abiding city.

Thomas a Kempis, Imitation of Christ

## Pilgrim Prayer of St. James

O God, who brought your servant Abraham
  out of the land of the Chaldeans,
    protecting him in his wandering across the desert, we ask
    that you watch over us, your servants, as we walk in the love
    of your name to Santiago.
Be for us our companion on the walk,
Our guide at the crossroads,
Our breath in our weariness,
Our protection in danger,
Our home on the Camino,
Our shade in the heat,
Our light in the darkness,
Our consolation in our discouragements, And our strength in
  our intentions.
So that with your guidance we may arrive safe and sound at the
  end of the road and enriched with grace and virtue we return
  safely to our homes filled with joy. In the name of Jesus
  Christ our Lord, Amen.

## Silent Prayer

## The Lord's Prayer

## Blessing

May the peace of the Lord Christ go with you,
Wherever he may guide you.
May he guide you through the wilderness,
Protect you through the storm.
May he bring you home rejoicing
At the wonders he has shown you.
May he bring you home rejoicing
Once again into our doors.

# SUNDAY MID-DAY

**Invitation**

For everything there is a season, and a time for every matter under heaven:
a time to be born, and a time to die;
a time to plant, and a time to pluck up what is planted;
a time to kill, and a time to heal;
a time to break down, and a time to build up;
a time to weep, and a time to laugh;
a time to mourn, and a time to dance;
a time to throw away stones, and a time to gather stones together;
a time to embrace, and a time to refrain from embracing;
a time to seek, and a time to lose;
a time to keep, and a time to throw away;
a time to tear, and a time to sew;
a time to keep silence, and a time to speak;
a time to love, and a time to hate;
a time for war, and a time for peace.

Ecclesiastes 3:1-8

**Lesson**

Once while Jesus was standing beside the lake of Gennesaret, and the crowd was pressing in on him to hear the word of God, he saw two boats there at the shore of the lake; the fishermen had gone out of them and were washing their nets. He got into one of the boats, the one belonging to Simon, and asked him to put out a little way from the shore. Then he sat down and taught the crowds from the boat. When he had finished speaking, he said to Simon, "Put out into the deep water and let down your nets for a catch." Simon answered, "Master, we have worked all night long but have caught nothing. Yet if you say so, I will let down the nets." When they had done this, they caught so many fish that their nets were beginning to break. So they signaled their partners in the other boat to come and help them. And they came and filled both boats, so that they began to sink. But when Simon Peter saw it, he fell down at Jesus' knees, saying, "Go away from me, Lord, for I am a sinful man!" For he and all who were with him were amazed at the catch of fish that they had taken; and so also were James and John, sons of Zebedee, who were partners with Simon. Then Jesus said to Simon, "Do not be afraid; from now on you will be catching people."

Luke 5:1-10

## Thanksgiving

Holy God,
We are grateful for all the possibilities of the pilgrim trail. We are grateful for simple nourishment and crisp clean water. We are grateful for the companionship of strangers, and the guiding presence of your Spirit. In Christ's name, Amen.

## Blessing

The human mind plans the way, but the Lord directs the steps.

Proverbs 16:9

# SUNDAY EVENING

### Invitation

Blessed be the God and Father of our Lord Jesus Christ! By his great mercy he has given us a new birth into a living hope through the resurrection of Jesus Christ from the dead, and into an inheritance that is imperishable, undefiled, and unfading, kept in heaven for you, who are being protected by the power of God through faith for a salvation ready to be revealed in the last time.

1 Peter 1:3-5

### Psalm

Bless the Lord, O my soul,
    and all that is within me,
    bless his holy name.
Bless the Lord, O my soul and do not forget all his benefits—
    who forgives all your iniquity,
    who heals all your diseases,
    who redeems your life from the Pit,
    who crowns you with steadfast love and mercy,
    who satisfies you with good as long as you live
    so that your youth is renewed like the eagle's.
The Lord works vindication and justice for all who are oppressed.
He made known his ways to Moses,
    his acts to the people of Israel.

The Lord is merciful and gracious,
> slow to anger and abounding in steadfast love.

Psalm 103:1-8

## Collect

O Holy God who brings all weary pilgrims to our true home with you. Guide our steps on your true path, strengthen us when we falter, inspire us with the tug of your Spirit, through Jesus Christ our redeemer and healer, Amen.

## Lesson

A Samaritan woman came to draw water, and Jesus said to her, "Give me a drink." His disciples had gone to the city to buy food. The Samaritan woman said to him, "How is it that you, a Jew, ask a drink of me, a woman of Samaria?" Jews do not share things in common with Samaritans. Jesus answered her, "If you knew the gift of God, and who it is that is saying to you, 'Give me a drink,' you would have asked him, and he would have given you living water." The woman said to him, "Sir, you have no bucket, and the well is deep. Where do you get that living water? Are you greater than our ancestor Jacob, who gave us the well, and with his sons and his flocks drank from it?" Jesus said to her, "Everyone who drinks of this water will be thirsty again, but those who drink of the water that I will give them will never be thirsty. The water that I will give will become in them a spring of water gushing up to eternal life." The woman said to him, "Sir, give me this water, so that I may never be thirsty or have to keep coming here to draw water."

John 4:7-15

## Reflection

Judging others makes us blind, whereas love is illuminating. By judging others we blind ourselves to our own evil and to the grace which others are just as entitled to as we are.

Dietrich Bonhoeffer, *The Cost of Discipleship*

## Prayer

Loving God,
The hardness of the pilgrim path makes me realize that we need you so much. Alone we tire, we falter, we break. Only with your help can we survive, thrive. And so we give ourselves to you. May we find joy on the road, discover something new, find our help and our care in you. Amen.

## Silent Prayer

## The Lord's Prayer

## Blessing

I can do all this through him who gives me strength.

Philippians 4:13

# MONDAY MORNING

## Invitation

I will put my spirit within you, and you shall live, and I will place you on your own soil; then you shall know that I, the Lord, have spoken and will act.

Ezekiel 37:14

## Psalm

I will extol you, my God and King,
    and bless your name forever and ever.
Every day I will bless you,
    and praise your name forever and ever.
Great is the Lord, and greatly to be praised;
The Lord is gracious and merciful,
    slow to anger and abounding in steadfast love.
The Lord is good to all,
    and his compassion is over all that he has made.
Your kingdom is an everlasting kingdom,
    and your dominion endures throughout all generations.
The Lord is faithful in all his words,
    and gracious in all his deeds.
The Lord upholds all who are falling,
    and raises up all who are bowed down.

Psalm 145:1-3, 8-9, 13-14

## Collect

Almighty and all-loving God, Creator of the universe and Sustainer of all things, grant that we would discover you in our sighs that are too deep for words, our breathing on the long trek towards you, the inspiration that can only come from you, our Lord Jesus Christ and with the power of the Holy Spirit, one God, who abounds in steadfast love, Amen.

## Lesson

Ask, and it will be given you; search, and you will find; knock, and the door will be opened for you. For everyone who asks receives, and everyone who searches finds, and for everyone who knocks, the door will be opened. Is there anyone among you who, if your child asks for bread, will give a stone? Or if the child asks for a fish, will give a snake? If you then, who are evil, know how to give good gifts to your children, how much more will your Father in heaven give good things to those who ask him!
"In everything do to others as you would have them do to you; for this is the law and the prophets.

Matthew 7:7-12

## Reflection

May today there be peace within. May you trust God that you are exactly where you are meant to be. May you not forget the infinite possibilities that are born of faith. May you use those gifts that you have received, and pass on the love that has been given to you. May you be content knowing you are a child of God. Let this presence settle into your bones, and allow your soul the freedom to sing, dance, praise and love. It is there for each and every one of us.

Teresa of Ávila, Interior Castle

## Prayer

Holy God,
We are your children. Although at times we are lost and the way is unclear, comfort us in the knowledge that we are exactly where we need to be. Our true home is always forever with you. Comfort us in the knowledge that in you, we are always found. Guide us on the path, for we need you so. Amen.

## Silent Prayer

## The Lord's Prayer

## Blessing

Let nothing disturb thee;
Nothing affright thee;
All things are passing;
God never changeth
Patience endurance attaneth all things:
Who God possesseth
In nothing is wanting;
Alone God sufficeth.

# MONDAY MID-DAY

**Invitation**

In the beginning was the Word, and the Word was with God, and the Word was God. He was in the beginning with God. All things came into being through him, and without him not one thing came into being. What has come into being in him was life, and the life was the light of all people. The light shines in the darkness, and the darkness did not overcome it.

John 1:1-5

**Lesson**

Jesus took with him Peter and James and his brother John and led them up a high mountain, by themselves. And he was transfigured before them, and his face shone like the sun, and his clothes became dazzling white. Suddenly there appeared to them Moses and Elijah, talking with him. Then Peter said to Jesus, "Lord, it is good for us to be here; if you wish, I will make three dwellings here, one for you, one for Moses, and one for Elijah." While he was still speaking, suddenly a bright cloud overshadowed them, and from the cloud a voice said, "This is my Son, the Beloved; with him I am well pleased; listen to him!" When the disciples heard this, they fell to the ground and were overcome by fear. But Jesus came and touched them, saying, "Get up and do not be afraid." And when they looked up, they saw no one except Jesus himself alone.

Matthew 17:1-8

## Thanksgiving

Loving God,
From the high peaks of the trail, may we behold you in your glory—the blazing sun, the green vista, the ribbon of trail that stretches on and on. Like those disciples who followed Jesus up the mountain, may this pilgrimage strengthen us in our faith, our values, and our devotion. From these many steps, we realize anew what we have known in my heart all along: you love us and all this world. We are your grateful servants. Amen.

## Blessing

The human mind may devise many plans, but it is the purpose of the Lord that will be established.

Proverbs 19:21

# MONDAY EVENING

### Invitation

For I know the plans I have for you," declares the Lord, "Plans to prosper you and not to harm you, plans to give you hope and a future."

Jeremiah 29:11

### Psalm

Blessed be the Lord,
    for he has heard the sound of my pleadings.
The Lord is my strength and my shield;
    in him my heart trusts;
so I am helped, and my heart exults,
    and with my song I give thanks to him.
The Lord is the strength of his people;
    he is the saving refuge of his anointed.
O save your people, and bless your heritage;
    be their shepherd, and carry them forever.

Psalm 28:6-9

## Collect

O Holy God, who stretches the trail through the mountains and draws all people towards you. Grant that you would sustain our hearts, strengthen our bodies, and encourage our minds, so that, in each step, we may move ever closer towards you, through Jesus Christ, your Son, who lives and reigns with you in the unity of the Holy Spirit, one God, for ever and ever. Amen.

## Lesson

Now all the tax collectors and sinners were coming near to listen to him. And the Pharisees and the scribes were grumbling and saying, "This fellow welcomes sinners and eats with them." So he told them this parable: "Which one of you, having a hundred sheep and losing one of them, does not leave the ninety-nine in the wilderness and go after the one that is lost until he finds it? When he has found it, he lays it on his shoulders and rejoices. And when he comes home, he calls together his friends and neighbors, saying to them, "Rejoice with me, for I have found my sheep that was lost." Just so, I tell you, there will be more joy in heaven over one sinner who repents than over ninety-nine righteous persons who need no repentance.

Luke 15:1-7

## Reflection

Believe in a love that is being stored up for you like an inheritance, and have faith that in this love there is a strength and a blessing so large that you can travel as far as you wish without having to step outside it.

Rainer Maria Rilke

## Prayer

Loving God,
We are grateful that we found our home today, the happy relief, the joyous reception of strangers, a cold drink, and a safe place to lay one's head. You seek us out on the pilgrim trail, and guide us on the way. We are grateful that we have our true home with you. In Christ's name, Amen.

## Silent Prayer

## The Lord's Prayer

## Blessing

I can do all this through him who gives me strength.

Philippians 4:13

# TUESDAY MORNING

## Invitation

Arise, shine; for your light has come,
  and the glory of the Lord has risen upon you.
For darkness shall cover the earth,
  and thick darkness the peoples;
but the Lord will arise upon you,
  and his glory will appear over you.

Isaiah 60:1

## Psalm

You who live in the shelter of the Most High,
    who abide in the shadow of the Almighty,
    will say to the Lord, "My refuge and my fortress;
    my God, in whom I trust."
You will not fear the terror of the night,
    or the arrow that flies by day,
Because you have made the Lord your refuge,
    the Most High your dwelling place,
    no evil shall befall you,
    no scourge come near your tent.
For he will command his angels concerning you
    to guard you in all your ways.

On their hands they will bear you up,
> so that you will not dash your foot against a stone.

Those who love me, I will deliver;
> I will protect those who know my name.

When they call to me, I will answer them;
> I will be with them in trouble,
> I will rescue them and honor them.

With long life I will satisfy them,
> and show them my salvation.

Psalm 91:1-2, 9-12, 14-16

## Collect

Holy God of light, love, and healing, help us, in our own brokenness, to behold you in the presence of others—their voices, their eyes, their bodies. Embolden us, with each step, to stretch our vision, reach out in trust, to the stranger, the lonely, the hurting, with the grace of our Lord Jesus and the help of the Holy Spirit, one God, Amen.

## Lesson

When Jesus had come down from the mountain, great crowds followed him; and there was a leper who came to him and knelt before him, saying, "Lord, if you choose, you can make me clean." He stretched out his hand and touched him, saying, "I do choose. Be made clean!" Immediately his leprosy was cleansed. Then Jesus said to him, "See that you say nothing to anyone; but go, show yourself to the priest, and offer the gift that Moses commanded, as a testimony to them."

Matthew 8:1-4

## Reflection

My soul's house is narrow for you to enter. Will you not make it broader? It is in a state of collapse. Will you not rebuild it? It contains things which must offend your eyes. This I know and admit. But who will make it clean?

Augustine, Confessions

## Prayer

Loving God,
We embark this morning on a journey to find our true home with you. Guide our feet on your way. Repair us of our brokenness. Inspire us to see your image in the eyes of those whom we meet. Keep us strong on the trail, for we need you so. Amen.

## Silent Prayer

## The Lord's Prayer

## Blessing

God to enfold me
God to surround me
God in my speaking
God in my thinking

God in my sleeping
God in my waking
God in my watching
God in my hoping

God in my life
God in my lips
God in my soul
God in my heart

God in my sufficing
God in my slumber
God in mine ever-living soul
God in mine eternity

# TUESDAY MID-DAY

**Invitation**

Those who hope in the Lord will renew their strength. They will soar on wings like eagles; they will run and not grow weary, they will walk and not be faint.

Isaiah 40:31

**Lesson**

While he was still speaking, some people came from the leader's house to say, "Your daughter is dead. Why trouble the teacher any further?" But overhearing what they said, Jesus said to the leader of the synagogue, "Do not fear, only believe." He allowed no one to follow him except Peter, James, and John, the brother of James. When they came to the house of the leader of the synagogue, he saw a commotion, people weeping and wailing loudly. When he had entered, he said to them, "Why do you make a commotion and weep? The child is not dead but sleeping." And they laughed at him. Then he put them all outside, and took the child's father and mother and those who were with him, and went in where the child was. He took her by the hand and said to her, "Talitha cum," which means, "Little girl, get up!" And immediately the girl got up and began to walk about (she was twelve years of age). At this they were overcome with amazement. He strictly ordered them that no one should know this, and told them to give her something to eat.

Mark 5:35-43

## Thanksgiving

Holy God,
Awaken us this morning. Through the valleys and over the hills, keep our spirits up. Amidst the busyness of life, keep our hearts simple. With all that is going on, help us to hold you at the center. Thank you so much for the richness of life—for friendships, for travel, for joy, for love. We are grateful for all of it, Amen.

## Blessing

In all your ways, acknowledge him, and he will make your paths straight.

Proverbs 3:6

# TUESDAY EVENING

## Invitation

A scribe then approached and said, "Teacher, I will follow you wherever you go." And Jesus said to him, "Foxes have holes, and birds of the air have nests; but the Son of Man has nowhere to lay his head."

Matthew 8:20

## Psalm

Protect me, O God, for in you I take refuge.
I bless the Lord who gives me counsel;
    in the night also my heart instructs me.
I keep the Lord always before me;
    because he is at my right hand, I shall not be moved.
Therefore my heart is glad, and my soul rejoices;
    my body also rests secure.
For you do not give me up to Sheol,
    or let your faithful one see the Pit.
You show me the path of life.
In your presence there is fullness of joy;

Psalm 16:1, 7-11

## Collect

Eternal and loving God who creates this land of such beauty and majesty and reconciles all the broken hearts to you, move in us with your Spirit that we could encourage hope among those who doubt, comfort to those who despair, and joy to those who falter, through Jesus Christ who lives and reigns with you, now and forever, Amen.

## Lesson

When Jesus saw the crowds, he went up the mountain; and after he sat down, his disciples came to him. Then he began to speak, and taught them, saying:
"Blessed are the poor in spirit, for theirs is the kingdom of heaven.
Blessed are those who mourn, for they will be comforted.
Blessed are the meek, for they will inherit the earth.
Blessed are those who hunger and thirst for righteousness, for they will be filled.
Blessed are the merciful, for they will receive mercy.
Blessed are the pure in heart, for they will see God.
Blessed are the peacemakers, for they will be called children of God....
You are the light of the world. A city built on a hill cannot be hid. No one after lighting a lamp puts it under the bushel basket, but on the lampstand, and it gives light to all in the house. In the same way, let your light shine before others, so that they may see your good works and give glory to your Father in heaven."

Matthew 5:1-9, 14-16

## Reflection

People are often unreasonable, irrational, and self-centered. Forgive them anyway. If you are kind, people may accuse you of

selfish, ulterior motives. Be kind anyway. If you are successful, you will win some unfaithful friends and some genuine enemies. Succeed anyway. If you are honest and sincere people may deceive you. Be honest and sincere anyway. What you spend years creating, others could destroy overnight. Create anyway.
If you find serenity and happiness, some may be jealous. Be happy anyway.

The good you do today, will often be forgotten. Do good anyway. Give the best you have, and it will never be enough. Give your best anyway.
In the final analysis, it is between you and God. It was never between you and them anyway.

Mother Teresa of Calcutta

### Prayer

Holy God,
You give strength to our steps and keep our spirits strong. You keep us safe and guide us in your way. We hunger and thirst for righteousness, for peace, for you. We are glad that you greet us on the trail. May your light shine through us for all the world. In Christ's name, amen.

### Silent Prayer

### The Lord's Prayer

### Blessing

I pray that, according to the riches of his glory, he may grant that you may be strengthened in your inner being with power through his Spirit, and that Christ may dwell in your hearts through faith, as you are being rooted and grounded in love. I pray that you may have the power to comprehend, with all the saints, what is the breadth and length and height and depth, and to know the love of Christ that surpasses knowledge, so that you may be filled with all the fullness of God.

Ephesians 3:16-19

# WEDNESDAY MORNING

### Invitation

For now we see through a glass, darkly; but then face to face: now I know in part; but then shall I know even as also I am known.

I Corinthians 13:12

### Psalm

O Lord my God, I cried to you for help,
    and you have healed me.
O Lord, you brought up my soul from Sheol,
    restored me to life from among those gone down to the Pit.
Sing praises to the Lord, O you his faithful ones,
    and give thanks to his holy name.
Hear, O Lord, and be gracious to me!
O Lord, be my helper!"
You have turned my mourning into dancing;
    you have taken off my sackcloth
    and clothed me with joy,
        so that my soul may praise you and not be silent.
O Lord my God, I will give thanks to you forever.

Psalm 30:2-4, 10-12

## Collect

Loving God, who makes all things holy, bless our rucksacks and boots, our backs and our legs, that every step might be a song of praise, every breath a prayer of thanksgiving, that you would guide us in safety to our destination which will be a foretaste of your heavenly kingdom of heaven which will fully come on earth, in the name of our Lord Jesus Christ and with the power of the Holy Spirit, one God, Amen.

## Lesson

He entered Jericho and was passing through it. A man was there named Zacchaeus; he was a chief tax collector and was rich. He was trying to see who Jesus was, but on account of the crowd he could not, because he was short in stature. So he ran ahead and climbed a sycamore tree to see him, because he was going to pass that way. When Jesus came to the place, he looked up and said to him, "Zacchaeus, hurry and come down; for I must stay at your house today." So he hurried down and was happy to welcome him. All who saw it began to grumble and said, "He has gone to be the guest of one who is a sinner." Zacchaeus stood there and said to the Lord, "Look, half of my possessions, Lord, I will give to the poor; and if I have defrauded anyone of anything, I will pay back four times as much." Then Jesus said to him, "Today salvation has come to this house, because he too is a son of Abraham. For the Son of Man came to seek out and to save the lost."

Luke 19:1-10

## Reflection

We ought not to be weary of doing little things for the love of God, who regards not the greatness of the work, but the love with which it is performed.

Brother Lawrence

### Prayer

Loving God,
We give our whole selves to you. Let your will be done. May our words, our deeds, be a reflection of your will. We are your instruments, and no task is too small. We pray for the strength to live this out, on the pilgrim trail and in our lives. In Christ's name, Amen.

### Silent Prayer

### The Lord's Prayer

### Blessing

May your past be a pleasant memory
Your future filled with delight and mystery
Your now a glorious moment
That fills your life with deep contentment

# WEDNESDAY MID-DAY

**Invitation**

For I am convinced that neither death nor life, neither angels nor demons, neither the present nor the future, nor any powers, neither height nor depth, nor anything else in all creation, will be able to separate us from the love of God that is in Christ Jesus our Lord.

Romans 8:38-39

**Lesson**

James and John, the sons of Zebedee, came forward to him and said to him, "Teacher, we want you to do for us whatever we ask of you." And he said to them, "What is it you want me to do for you?" And they said to him, "Grant us to sit, one at your right hand and one at your left, in your glory." But Jesus said to them, "You do not know what you are asking. Are you able to drink the cup that I drink, or be baptized with the baptism that I am baptized with?" They replied, "We are able." Then Jesus said to them, "The cup that I drink you will drink; and with the baptism with which I am baptized, you will be baptized; but to sit at my right hand or at my left is not mine to grant, but it is for those for whom it has been prepared."

When the ten heard this, they began to be angry with James and John. So Jesus called them and said to them, "You know that among the Gentiles those whom they recognize as their rulers lord it over them, and their great ones are tyrants over them. But it is not so among you; but whoever wishes to become great among you must be your servant, and whoever wishes to be first among you must be slave of all. For the Son of Man came not to be served but to serve, and to give his life a ransom for many."

Mark 10:35-45

## Thanksgiving

Loving God,
We venture on the pilgrim trail not for glory, but as a service of devotion. We are grateful that you stitch our muscles together each day, and fill our lungs with mountain air. We know not where we will sleep this night, but trust that we will always have our home with you. Be with us on the trail for we need you so. In Christ's name, Amen.

## Blessing

Rich and poor have this in common: The Lord is the Maker of them all.

Proverbs 22:2

# WEDNESDAY EVENING

**Invitation**

Even to your old age and gray hairs I am he, I am he who will sustain you. I have made you and I will carry you; I will sustain you and I will rescue you.

Isaiah 46:4

**Psalm**

O Lord, our Sovereign,
    how majestic is your name in all the earth!
You have set your glory above the heavens.
Out of the mouths of babes and infants
    you have founded a bulwark because of your foes,
to silence the enemy and the avenger.
When I look at your heavens, the work of your fingers,
    the moon and the stars that you have established;
    what are human beings that you are mindful of them,
    mortals that you care for them?
Yet you have made them a little lower than God,
    and crowned them with glory and honor.
You have given them dominion over the works of your hands;
    you have put all things under their feet,
        all sheep and oxen,
and also the beasts of the field,

the birds of the air, and the fish of the sea,
whatever passes along the paths of the seas.
O Lord, our Sovereign,
>     how majestic is your name in all the earth!

*Psalm 8:1-9*

## Collect

Eternal God of love and peace, who protects pilgrims and all who seek you, accompany us as we navigate the complex paths of our age. Turn our deepest desires towards you. Kindle in us a spark that would become a fire that burns for you and renews your creation, through Jesus Christ our Lord, who with you and the Holy Spirit lives and reigns, one God, for ever and ever. Amen.

## Lesson

The disciples of John reported all these things to him. So John summoned two of his disciples and sent them to the Lord to ask, "Are you the one who is to come, or are we to wait for another?" When the men had come to him, they said, "John the Baptist has sent us to you to ask, 'Are you the one who is to come, or are we to wait for another?'" Jesus had just then cured many people of diseases, plagues, and evil spirits, and had given sight to many who were blind. And he answered them, "Go and tell John what you have seen and heard: the blind receive their sight, the lame walk, the lepers are cleansed, the deaf hear, the dead are raised, the poor have good news brought to them.

*Luke 7:18-22*

## Reflection

"Jesus becomes more like us, so that we can become more like him."

William Sloane Coffin

## Prayer

Loving God,
We are grateful for a good night's rest, a hot shower, a delicious meal, a soft bed. We are grateful to be together, grateful to be in your company. May what we learn on our pilgrimage shape our hearts forever. In Christ's name, Amen.

## Silent Prayer

## The Lord's Prayer

## Blessing

Let the peace of Christ rule in your hearts, to which indeed you were called in the one body. And be thankful. Let the word of Christ dwell in you richly; teach and admonish one another in all wisdom; and with gratitude in your hearts sing psalms, hymns, and spiritual songs to God. And whatever you do, in word or deed, do everything in the name of the Lord Jesus, giving thanks to God the Father through him.

Colossians 3:15-17

# THURSDAY MORNING

**Invitation**

Above all, love each other deeply, because love covers over a multitude of sins.

1 Peter 4:8

**Psalm**

Make a joyful noise to the Lord, all the earth.
Worship the Lord with gladness;
    come into his presence with singing.
Know that the Lord is God.
It is he that made us, and we are his;
    we are his people, and the sheep of his pasture.
Enter his gates with thanksgiving,
    and his courts with praise.
Give thanks to him, bless his name.
For the Lord is good;
    his steadfast love endures forever,
    and his faithfulness to all generations.

Psalm 100:1-5

## Collect

All powerful God, who shows mercy and kindness to all who seek you, guide your servants on this pilgrimage, that you would be a shelter amidst the storm, a strength in fatigue, a consolation amidst despair, a joy in our intentions, that we would arrive to your cathedral enriched by your Spirit, graced by Christ's presence, and made whole by your love, one God, for ever and ever. Amen.

## Lesson

Now on that same day two of them were going to a village called Emmaus, about seven miles from Jerusalem, and talking with each other about all these things that had happened. While they were talking and discussing, Jesus himself came near and went with them, but their eyes were kept from recognizing him.

As they came near the village to which they were going, he walked ahead as if he were going on. But they urged him strongly, saying, "Stay with us, because it is almost evening and the day is now nearly over." So he went in to stay with them. When he was at the table with them, he took bread, blessed and broke it, and gave it to them. Then their eyes were opened, and they recognized him; and he vanished from their sight. They said to each other, "Were not our hearts burning within us while he was talking to us on the road, while he was opening the scriptures to us?"

*Luke 24:13-16, 28-32*

## Reflection

I am the fiery life of the essence of God; I am the flame above the beauty in the fields; I shine in the waters; I burn in the sun, the moon, and the stars. And with the airy wind, I quicken all things vitally by an unseen, all-sustaining life.

Hildegard of Bingen

## Prayer

Loving God,
The sun has yet to crest the horizon. We are awake and ready to go. Thank you for healing sore muscles, for toughening blisters, for encouraging us in our weariness. Guide us today. Keep us safe. As we embark on our Emmaus road, may we discover you anew. Amen

## Silent Prayer

## The Lord's Prayer

## Blessing

May God shield me
May God fill me
May God keep me
May God watch me
May God bring me this night
To the nearness of His love

# THURSDAY MID-DAY

**Invitation**

He has shown you, O mortal, what is good. And what does the Lord require of you? To act justly and to love mercy and to walk humbly with your God.

Micah 6:8

**Lesson**

Then Jesus called the twelve together and gave them power and authority over all demons and to cure diseases, and he sent them out to proclaim the kingdom of God and to heal. He said to them, "Take nothing for your journey, no staff, nor bag, nor bread, nor money—not even an extra tunic. Whatever house you enter, stay there, and leave from there. Wherever they do not welcome you, as you are leaving that town shake the dust off your feet as a testimony against them." They departed and went through the villages, bringing the good news and curing diseases everywhere.

Luke 9:1-6

## Thanksgiving

Holy God,
We are grateful that we carry only what we need. Even then, it is often too much, for what we truly need can only be found in you. May we join your twelve in bringing good news to the world. In Christ's name, Amen.

## Blessing

Above all else, guard your heart, for everything you do flows from it.

Proverbs 4:23

# THURSDAY EVENING

**Invitation**

I appeal to you therefore, brothers and sisters, by the mercies of God, to present your bodies as a living sacrifice, holy and acceptable to God, which is your spiritual worship. Do not be conformed to this world, but be transformed by the renewing of your minds, so that you may discern what is the will of God—what is good and acceptable and perfect.

Romans 12:1-2

**Psalm**

O Lord, you have searched me and known me.
You know when I sit down and when I rise up;
    you discern my thoughts from far away.
You search out my path and my lying down,
    and are acquainted with all my ways.
If I ascend to heaven, you are there;
    if I make my bed in Sheol, you are there.
If I take the wings of the morning
    and settle at the farthest limits of the sea,
    even there your hand shall lead me,
    and your right hand shall hold me fast.
If I say, "Surely the darkness shall cover me,
    and the light around me become night,"

> even the darkness is not dark to you;
> the night is as bright as the day,
> for darkness is as light to you.

For it was you who formed my inward parts;
> you knit me together in my mother's womb.

I praise you, for I am fearfully and wonderfully made.

Psalms 139:1-3, 8-14

## Collect

Almighty God, the source of all life and motivation, grant us the strength to detach ourselves from needless possessions so we might journey with the lightness of joy and the freedom of discovery, in the company of your Son Jesus Christ, our Lord, and empowered by your Holy Spirit, on God, forever and ever, Amen.

## Lesson

In the beginning was the Word, and the Word was with God, and the Word was God. He was in the beginning with God. All things came into being through him, and without him not one thing came into being. What has come into being in him was life, and the life was the light of all people. The light shines in the darkness, and the darkness did not overcome it. There was a man sent from God, whose name was John. He came as a witness to testify to the light, so that all might believe through him. He himself was not the light, but he came to testify to the light. The true light, which enlightens everyone, was coming into the world.

He was in the world, and the world came into being through him; yet the world did not know him. He came to what was his own, and his own people did not accept him. But to all who received him, who believed in his name, he gave power to become children of God, who were born, not of blood or of the will of the flesh or of the will of man, but of God. And the Word became flesh and lived among us, and we have seen his glory, the glory as of a father's only son, full of grace and truth.

John 1:1-14

## Reflection

"For I tell you this: one loving, blind desire for God alone is more valuable in itself, more pleasing to God and to the saints, more beneficial to your own growth, and more helpful to your friends, both living and dead, than anything else you could do."

Anonymous, The Cloud of Unknowing

## Prayer

Loving God,
We commit to this path, one step after another, towards what? Only you know. Loosen us from those shackles of our lives that hold us back. Crack open those hard parts of our hearts so that we could behold the world with new eyes. O Loving God, grant us courage on this pilgrim way to be vulnerable to whatever your path may behold. We are ready. We take our first steps towards you, Amen.

## Silent Prayer

## The Lord's Prayer

## Blessing

Let love be genuine; hate what is evil, hold fast to what is good; love one another with mutual affection; outdo one another in showing honor. Do not lag in zeal, be ardent in spirit, serve the Lord. Rejoice in hope, be patient in suffering, persevere in prayer. Contribute to the needs of the saints; extend hospitality to strangers.

Romans 12:9-13

# FRIDAY MORNING

## Invitation

For through the law I died to the law, so that I might live to God. I have been crucified with Christ; and it is no longer I who live, but it is Christ who lives in me. And the life I now live in the flesh I live by faith in the Son of God, who loved me and gave himself for me.

Galatians 2:19-20

## Psalm

Hear, O Lord, when I cry aloud,
    be gracious to me and answer me!
"Come," my heart says, "seek his face!"
Your face, Lord, do I seek.
Do not hide your face from me.
Do not turn your servant away in anger,
    you who have been my help.
Do not cast me off, do not forsake me,
O God of my salvation!
    If my father and mother forsake me,
    the Lord will take me up.
Teach me your way, O Lord,
    and lead me on a level path
    because of my enemies.

Do not give me up to the will of my adversaries,
> for false witnesses have risen against me,
> and they are breathing out violence.
I believe that I shall see the goodness of the Lord
> in the land of the living.
Wait for the Lord;
> be strong, and let your heart take courage;
> wait for the Lord!

*Psalm 27:11-14*

## Collect

O merciful Creator, who reaches out to the lost, grant us vision to follow the true path, patience to forge ahead, and steadiness of spirit, that with a glad heart we would great you in the fullness of life, in the land of the living. Encourage us O loving God, in the name of our Lord Jesus and the Holy Spirit, one God, for ever and ever, Amen.

## Lesson

They came to Bethsaida, and some people brought a blind man and begged Jesus to touch him. He took the blind man by the hand and led him outside the village. When he had spit on the man's eyes and put his hands on him, Jesus asked, "Do you see anything?"
He looked up and said, "I see people; they look like trees walking around."
Once more Jesus put his hands on the man's eyes. Then his eyes were opened, his sight was restored, and he saw everything clearly.

*Mark 8:22-25*

## Reflection

The most beautiful things in the world cannot be seen or touched, they are felt with the heart.

> Antoine de Saint-Exupéry, The Little Prince

## Prayer

Loving God,
Thank you for keeping our legs strong, our spirits up. Thank you for your guidance on the pilgrim trail. Open our eyes, open our hearts, to your beauty in the world. Open our whole selves to your presence—that which we behold with our bodies, that which we feel in our hearts. We greet the sun on the road today. Keep our feet on your path. In Christ's name, Amen.

## Silent Prayer

## The Lord's Prayer

## Blessing

I arise today
Through a mighty strength
God's power to guide me
God's might to uphold me
God's eyes to watch over me
God's ear to hear me
God's word to give me speech
God's hand to guard me
God's way to lie before me
God's shield to shelter me
God's host to secure me

# FRIDAY MID-DAY

## Invitation

He has made everything beautiful in its time. He has also set eternity in the human heart; yet no one can fathom what God has done from beginning to end.

Ecclesiastes 3:11

## Lesson

While staying with them, he ordered them not to leave Jerusalem, but to wait there for the promise of the Father. "This," he said, "is what you have heard from me; for John baptized with water, but you will be baptized with the Holy Spirit not many days from now."

So when they had come together, they asked him, "Lord, is this the time when you will restore the kingdom to Israel?" He replied, "It is not for you to know the times or periods that the Father has set by his own authority. But you will receive power when the Holy Spirit has come upon you; and you will be my witnesses in Jerusalem, in all Judea and Samaria, and to the ends of the earth." When he had said this, as they were watching, he was lifted up, and a cloud took him out of their sight. While he was going and they were gazing up toward heaven, suddenly two men in white robes stood by them. They said, "Men of Galilee, why do you stand looking up toward heaven? This Jesus, who has been taken up from you into heaven, will come in the same way as you saw him go into heaven."

Then they returned to Jerusalem from the mount called Olivet, which is near Jerusalem, a sabbath day's journey away. When they had entered the city, they went to the room upstairs where they were staying, Peter, and John, and James, and Andrew, Philip and Thomas, Bartholomew and Matthew, James son of Alphaeus, and Simon the Zealot, and Judas son of James. All these were constantly devoting themselves to prayer, together with certain women, including Mary the mother of Jesus, as well as his brothers.

Acts 1:3-14

## Thanksgiving

Loving God,
We walk the lonely trail. We sweat. We ache. We discover you anew in this adventure. You have been with us all along in our struggles. Our blisters, our thirst, our aching joints. There is joy in all this because it is an offering of hope. The trail beckons. O loving God, guide us. Amen.

## Blessing

The fear of the Lord is the beginning of wisdom, and knowledge of the Holy One is understanding.

Proverbs 9:10

# FRIDAY EVENING

## Invitation

Then I heard the voice of the Lord saying, "Whom shall I send, and who will go for us?" And I said, "Here am I; send me!"

Isaiah 6:8

## Psalm

I lift up my eyes to the hills—
    rom where will my help come?
My help comes from the Lord,
    who made heaven and earth.
He will not let your foot be moved;
    he who keeps you will not slumber.
He who keeps Israel
    will neither slumber nor sleep.
The Lord is your keeper;
    the Lord is your shade at your right hand.
The sun shall not strike you by day,
    nor the moon by night.
The Lord will keep you from all evil;
    he will keep your life.

The Lord will keep
>your going out and your coming in
>from this time on and forevermore.

Psalm 121

## Collect

Holy God, the alpha and omega, who knows our beginning and our end, attune our ears to hear your call, open our eyes to behold your grace, inspire our minds to discern your presence, strengthen our whole selves that, whatever we may encounter, we may reflect your presence in the world, with the help of Jesus Christ our Lord and the power of the Holy Spirit, Amen.

## Lesson

Then some people came, bringing to him a paralyzed man, carried by four of them. And when they could not bring him to Jesus because of the crowd, they removed the roof above him; and after having dug through it, they let down the mat on which the paralytic lay. When Jesus saw their faith, he said to the paralytic, "Son, your sins are forgiven." Now some of the scribes were sitting there, questioning in their hearts, "Why does this fellow speak in this way? It is blasphemy! Who can forgive sins but God alone?" At once Jesus perceived in his spirit that they were discussing these questions among themselves; and he said to them, "Why do you raise such questions in your hearts? Which is easier, to say to the paralytic, 'Your sins are forgiven,' or to say, 'Stand up and take your mat and walk'? But so that you may know that the Son of Man has authority on earth to forgive sins"—he said to the paralytic— "I say to you, stand up, take your mat and go to your home." And he stood up, and immediately took the mat and went out before all of them; so that they were all amazed and glorified God, saying, "We have never seen anything like this!"

Mark 2:3-12

## Reflection

Give me my scallop shell of quiet,
My staff of faith to walk upon,
My scrip of joy, immortal diet,
My bottle of salvation,
My gown of glory, hope's true gage,
And thus I'll take my pilgrimage.

> Sir Walter Ralegh, The Passionate Man's Pilgrimage

## Prayer

Loving God,
You guided us through the dark morning, gave strength to our legs, and led us to a warm bed, good food, a hot shower. We are so grateful for the adventure of the trail, and the deep joy of good rest. Thank you for seeing us through. We are grateful. We love you. Amen.

## Silent Prayer

## The Lord's Prayer

## Blessing

Have I not commanded you? Be strong and courageous. Do not be afraid; do not be discouraged, for the Lord your God will be with you wherever you go.

> Joshua 1:9

# SATURDAY MORNING

**Invitation**

Call to me and I will answer you, and will tell you great and hidden things that you have not known.

Jeremiah 33:3

**Psalm**

God is our refuge and strength,
    a very present help in trouble.
Therefore we will not fear, though the earth should change,
    though the mountains shake in the heart of the sea;
    though its waters roar and foam,
    though the mountains tremble with its tumult.
There is a river whose streams make glad the city of God,
    the holy habitation of the Most High.
God is in the midst of the city; it shall not be moved;
    God will help it when the morning dawns.
The nations are in an uproar, the kingdoms totter;
    he utters his voice, the earth melts.
The Lord of hosts is with us;
    the God of Jacob is our refuge.
Come, behold the works of the Lord;
    see what desolations he has brought on the earth.

He makes wars cease to the end of the earth;
> he breaks the bow, and shatters the spear;
> he burns the shields with fire.

"Be still, and know that I am God!
> I am exalted among the nations,
> I am exalted in the earth."

The Lord of hosts is with us;
> the God of Jacob is our refuge.

Psalm 46:1-11

## Collect

Creator God of mountains and rivers, of dreams and aspirations, move in us this morning as we trod upon the pilgrim path, that we would discover your peace in the stillness of the morning, that we would find our true joy with you on the trail, and find our good rest in your arms this eve, with the help of our Lord Jesus Christ and the encouragement of the Holy Spirit, one God, in true love, Amen.

## Lesson

And Mary said,
"My soul magnifies the Lord,
> and my spirit rejoices in God my Savior,
> for he has looked with favor on the lowliness of his servant.

Surely, from now on all generations will call me blessed;
> for the Mighty One has done great things for me,
> and holy is his name.

His mercy is for those who fear him
> from generation to generation.

He has shown strength with his arm;
> he has scattered the proud in the thoughts of their hearts.

He has brought down the powerful from their thrones,
> and lifted up the lowly;

he has filled the hungry with good things,
    and sent the rich away empty.
He has helped his servant Israel,
    in remembrance of his mercy,
        according to the promise he made to our ancestors,
    to Abraham and to his descendants forever."

Luke 1:46-55

## Reflection

The glory of God is humanity fully alive.

Ireneaus

## Prayer

Loving God,
Thank you for being with us in the dawn, for nudging us out of bed. Thank you for your company, your guidance. We are grateful that you have brought us this far. Keep our legs strong, our backs straight, our spirits high. On the trail we disover you anew. And there is more trail, more of you, to discover. O God, I love you, Amen.

## Silent Prayer

## The Lord's Prayer

## Blessing

Christ, as light, illumine and guide me
Christ, as a shield, overshadow me
Christ under me
Christ over me
Christ beside me
On my left and my right

## SATURDAY MORNING

This day be within and without me
Lowly and meek yet all-powerful
Be in the heart of each to whom I speak
In the mouth of each who speaks unto me
This day be within and without me
Lowly and meek, yet all powerful
Christ as a light
Christ as a shield
Christ beside me
On my left and on my right

# SATURDAY MID-DAY

**Invitation**

Beloved, let us love one another, because love is from God; everyone who loves is born of God and knows God. Whoever does not love does not know God, for God is love. God's love was revealed among us in this way: God sent his only Son into the world so that we might live through him.

I John 4:7-8

**Lesson**

When the day of Pentecost had come, they were all together in one place. And suddenly from heaven there came a sound like the rush of a violent wind, and it filled the entire house where they were sitting. Divided tongues, as of fire, appeared among them, and a tongue rested on each of them. All of them were filled with the Holy Spirit and began to speak in other languages, as the Spirit gave them ability.

But Peter, standing with the eleven, raised his voice and addressed them, "Men of Judea and all who live in Jerusalem, let this be known to you, and listen to what I say. Indeed, these are not drunk, as you suppose, for it is only nine o'clock in the morning. No, this is what was spoken through the prophet Joel:

'In the last days it will be, God declares,
that I will pour out my Spirit upon all flesh,
 and your sons and your daughters shall prophesy,
 and your young men shall see visions,
 and your old men shall dream dreams.
Even upon my slaves, both men and women,
 in those days I will pour out my Spirit; and they shall prophesy.
And I will show portents in the heaven above
 and signs on the earth below, blood, and fire, and smoky mist.
The sun shall be turned to darkness and the moon to blood,
 before the coming of the Lord's great and glorious day.
Then everyone who calls on the name of the Lord shall be saved.'

Acts 2:1-6, 14-21

## Thanksgiving

Holy God,
We are grateful for visions of hope, dreams of possibility, for these are the gifts of your Spirit. Open our eyes to the signs of your coming, for the glorious day when we shall be saved, when we shall find our true home with you. In Christ's name, Amen.

## Blessing

Commit your work to the Lord, and your plans will be established.

Proverbs 16:3

# SATURDAY EVENING

**Invitation**

For I know the plans I have for you," declares the LORD, "plans to prosper you and not to harm you, plans to give you hope and a future.

Jeremiah 29:11

**Psalm**

I love you, O Lord, my strength.
The Lord is my rock, my fortress, and my deliverer,
    my God, my rock in whom I take refuge,
        my shield, and the horn of my salvation, my stronghold.
I call upon the Lord, who is worthy to be praised,

For who is God except the Lord?
    and who is a rock besides our God?—
the God who girded me with strength,
and made my way safe.
He made my feet like the feet of a deer,
    and set me secure on the heights.

Psalm 18:1-3, 31-33

## Collect

Eternal God, our rock and our refuge, grant us the courage to trust in you for all that we need. Release us from guilt, lighten our burdens, embolden in us a love that stretches across the differences that divide us and draws us all together as one people, with the help of your Son Jesus Christ and the power of your Holy Spirit, one God, now and forever, Amen.

## Lesson

Then his father Zechariah was filled with the Holy Spirit and
 spoke this prophecy:
"Blessed be the Lord God of Israel,
 for he has looked favorably on his people and redeemed
 them.
He has raised up a mighty savior for us
 in the house of his servant David,
 as he spoke through the mouth of his holy prophets from of
 old,
 that we would be saved from our enemies and from the hand
 of all who hate us.
Thus he has shown the mercy promised to our ancestors,
 and has remembered his holy covenant,
 the oath that he swore to our ancestor Abraham,
 to grant us that we, being rescued from the hands of our
 enemies,
 might serve him without fear, in holiness and righteousness
 before him all our days.
And you, child, will be called the prophet of the Most High;
 for you will go before the Lord to prepare his ways,
 to give knowledge of salvation to his people
 by the forgiveness of their sins.
By the tender mercy of our God,
 the dawn from on high will break upon us,
 to give light to those who sit in darkness and in the shadow

of death,
to guide our feet into the way of peace."

Luke 1:67-79

## Reflection

The day will come when, after harnessing the ether, the winds, the tides, gravitation, we shall harness for God the energies of love. And, on that day, for the second time in the history of the world, man will have discovered fire.

Pierre Teilhard de Chardin, The Evolution of Chastity

## Prayer

Loving God,
Let your Spirit stitch together our weary muscles. Let your Spirit be a salve to our blisters. We are tired. The way is longer and harder than we thought. Keep us strong until the end of the trail, and whatever comes next. Amen.

## Silent Prayer

## The Lord's Prayer

## Blessing

For the Spirit God gave us does not make us timid, but gives us power, love and self-discipline.

2 Timothy 1:7

# COMPLINE
## ~ A prayer for the close of the day

### Invitation

Come to me, all you that are weary and are carrying heavy burdens, and I will give you rest. Take my yoke upon you, and learn from me; for I am gentle and humble in heart, and you will find rest for your souls. For my yoke is easy, and my burden is light.

*Matthew 11:28-30*

### Psalm

Have mercy on me, O God,
    according to your steadfast love;
    according to your abundant mercy
    blot out my transgressions.
Wash me thoroughly from my iniquity,
    and cleanse me from my sin.
Create in me a clean heart, O God,
    and put a new and right spirit within me.
Do not cast me away from your presence,
    and do not take your holy spirit from me.
Restore to me the joy of your salvation,
    and sustain in me a willing spirit.
Then I will teach transgressors your ways,
    and sinners will return to you.

Deliver me from bloodshed, O God,
 O God of my salvation.

Psalm 51:1-2, 10-14

## Confession

Dear God, I cannot love Thee the way I want to. You are the slim crescent of a moon that I see and myself is the earth's shadow that keeps me from seeing all the moon. What I am afraid of, dear God, is that myself shadow will grow so large that it blocks the whole moon, and that I will judge myself by the shadow that is nothing. I do not know you God because I am in the way. Please help me to push myself aside. I want very much to succeed in the world with what I want to do. I have prayed to you about this with my mind and strung my nerves into a tension and said, "oh God, please," and "I must," and "please, please." I have not asked you, I feel, in the right way. Let me henceforth ask You with resignation. I do not wish to presume. I want to love. Amen

Flannery O'Connor

## Assurance of Pardon

Therefore having been justified by faith, we have peace with God through our Lord Jesus Christ.

Romans 5:1

## Blessing

The Lord bless you and keep you; the Lord make his face shine on you and be gracious to you; the Lord turn his face toward you and give you peace.

Numbers 6:24-26

PRAYERS FOR THE DAY OF ARRIVAL
TO SANTIAGO DE COMPOSTELA

# MORNING

**Invitation**

This is the day that the Lord has made. Let us be glad and rejoice in it!

Psalm 118:4

**Psalm**

Clap your hands, all you peoples;
    shout to God with loud songs of joy.
For the Lord, the Most High, is awesome,
    a great king over all the earth.
He subdued peoples under us,
    and nations under our feet.
He chose our heritage for us,
    the pride of Jacob whom he loves.
God has gone up with a shout,
    the Lord with the sound of a trumpet.
Sing praises to God, sing praises;
    sing praises to our King, sing praises.
For God is the king of all the earth;

Psalm 47:1-7

## Collect

Almighty God, whom truly to know is everlasting life. Grant us so perfectly to know your Son Jesus Christ to be the way, the truth, and the life, that we may steadfastly follow his steps in the way that leads to eternal life; through Jesus Christ your Son our Lord, who lives and reigns with you in the unity of the Holy Spirit, one God, forever and ever. Amen.

## Lesson

Now a certain man was ill, Lazarus of Bethany, the village of Mary and her sister Martha. Mary was the one who anointed the Lord with perfume and wiped his feet with her hair; her brother Lazarus was ill. So the sisters sent a message to Jesus, "Lord, he whom you love is ill." But when Jesus heard it, he said, "This illness does not lead to death; rather it is for God's glory, so that the Son of God may be glorified through it."

When Jesus arrived, he found that Lazarus had already been in the tomb four days. Now Bethany was near Jerusalem, some two miles away, and many of the Jews had come to Martha and Mary to console them about their brother. When Martha heard that Jesus was coming, she went and met him, while Mary stayed at home. Martha said to Jesus, "Lord, if you had been here, my brother would not have died. But even now I know that God will give you whatever you ask of him." Jesus said to her, "Your brother will rise again." Martha said to him, "I know that he will rise again in the resurrection on the last day." Jesus said to her, "I am the resurrection and the life. Those who believe in me, even though they die, will live, and everyone who lives and believes in me will never die. Do you believe this?" She said to him, "Yes, Lord, I believe that you are the Messiah, the Son of God, the one coming into the world."

John 11:1-4, 17-27

## Reflection

Yea, if a man possesses all things he cannot be content — the greater his possessions the less will be his contentment, for the heart cannot be satisfied with possessions, but rather in detachment from all things and in poverty of spirit.

John of the Cross

## Prayer

Loving God,
We approach your cathedral with a poverty of spirit, living simply with our only possessions on our backs. We approach your cathedral with hearts open to your grace, grateful that you are with us on this journey and to the end of the age. May we discover you anew this day. Amen.

## Silent Prayer

## The Lord's Prayer

## Blessing

May the road rise up to meet you.
May the wind be always at your back.
May the sun shine warm upon your face;
the rains fall soft upon your fields and until we meet again, may God hold you in the palm of His hand.

PRAYERS FOR THE DAY OF ARRIVAL
TO SANTIAGO DE COMPOSTELA

# MID-DAY

**Invitation**

Have you not known? Have you not heard?
The Lord is the everlasting God,
    the Creator of the ends of the earth.
He does not faint or grow weary;
    his understanding is unsearchable.
He gives power to the faint,
    and strengthens the powerless.
Even youths will faint and be weary,
    and the young will fall exhausted;
    but those who wait for the Lord shall renew their strength,
    they shall mount up with wings like eagles,
    they shall run and not be weary,
    they shall walk and not faint.

Isaiah 40:28-31

**Lesson**

Rejoice in the Lord always; again I will say, Rejoice. Let your gentleness be known to everyone. The Lord is near. Do not worry about anything, but in everything by prayer and supplication with thanksgiving let your requests be made known to God. And the peace of God, which surpasses all understanding, will guard your hearts and your minds in Christ Jesus.

Finally, beloved, whatever is true, whatever is honorable, whatever is just, whatever is pure, whatever is pleasing, whatever is commendable, if there is any excellence and if there is anything worthy of praise, think about these things. Keep on doing the things that you have learned and received and heard and seen in me, and the God of peace will be with you.

Philippians 4:4-9

## Thanksgiving

Holy God,
We see the spires of your cathedral in the distance. We rejoice that our goal is near, but grieve too a bit that our adventure soon will end. Thank you for what we have discovered on your trail. We will always be your pilgrims. Keep us in the pilgrim way, always in the joy, the simplicity of the pilgrim way. In Christ's name, Amen.

## Blessing

May the God of hope fill you with all joy and peace in believing, so that you may abound in hope by the power of the Holy Spirit.

Romans 15:13

PRAYERS FOR THE DAY OF ARRIVAL
TO SANTIAGO DE COMPOSTELA

# EVENING

### Invitation

Jesus spoke to them, saying, "I am the light of the world. Whoever follows me will never walk in darkness but will have the light of life."

John 8:12

### Psalm

Praise the Lord, all you nations!
Extol him, all you peoples!
For great is his steadfast love toward us,
    and the faithfulness of the Lord endures forever.
Praise the Lord!

Psalm 117

### Collect

Eternal and Almighty God, who is with us unto the end of the age, give us courage and conviction that we may joyfully follow you from this Camino into new adventures of faith, service, and discovery, led by your Son Jesus Christ, the light of the world, and guided by your Holy Spirit, one God, forever and ever, Amen.

## Lesson

After the Sabbath, as the first day of the week was dawning, Mary Magdalene and the other Mary went to see the tomb. And suddenly there was a great earthquake; for an angel of the Lord, descending from heaven, came and rolled back the stone and sat on it. His appearance was like lightning, and his clothing white as snow. For fear of him the guards shook and became like dead men. But the angel said to the women, "Do not be afraid; I know that you are looking for Jesus who was crucified. He is not here; for he has been raised, as he said. Come, see the place where he lay. Then go quickly and tell his disciples, 'He has been raised from the dead, and indeed he is going ahead of you to Galilee; there you will see him.' This is my message for you." So they left the tomb quickly with fear and great joy, and ran to tell his disciples. Suddenly Jesus met them and said, "Greetings!" And they came to him, took hold of his feet, and worshiped him. Then Jesus said to them, "Do not be afraid; go and tell my brothers to go to Galilee; there they will see me."

Now the eleven disciples went to Galilee, to the mountain to which Jesus had directed them. When they saw him, they worshiped him; but some doubted. And Jesus came and said to them, "All authority in heaven and on earth has been given to me. Go therefore and make disciples of all nations, baptizing them in the name of the Father and of the Son and of the Holy Spirit, and teaching them to obey everything that I have commanded you. And remember, I am with you always, to the end of the age."

Matthew 28:1-10, 16-20

## Reflection

You can never learn that Christ is all you need, until Christ is all you have.

Corrie Ten Boom

## Prayer

Holy God,
We arrive weary and spent. We give ourselves to you for you have given yourself to us. Upon these cobblestones, surrounded by these grand spires, amidst the throngs of your people, we awaken to the reality that you are all that we need. May you shape us and use us for your purposes for the journey ahead. In Christ's name, Amen.

## Silent Prayer

## The Lord's Prayer

## Blessing

I have fought the good fight, I have finished the race, I have kept the faith. Now there is in store for me the crown of righteousness, which the Lord, the righteous Judge, will award to me on that day—and not only to me, but also to all who have longed for his appearing.

2 Timothy 4:7-8

"We have two lives. The second one begins when we discover we only have one."

~ a quote shared by a pilgrim on the trail